Secondhand Autism

By Paul Brodie

Text copyright © 2013 Paul Brodie

Cover design by Paul Brodie and Markus Hannonen

All photographs from family collection

All Rights Reserved

ISBN-13: 978-1482791037

For my parents and siblings:

It hasn't always been easy, in fact a lot of it has been outright difficult, but we've remained united, making our experience worth more than any of the sacrifices.

Left to right: Top step: Alison, John; Second step: Scott, Laura; Bottom step: Paul, Shannon. August 2008

Table of Contents

1. Introduction 1
2. Autism in my family 9
3. Autism's Effect on Parents 19
4. Autism's Effect on Siblings............33
5. Notes from My Siblings 43
6. Autism's Effect on me 53
7. The Secondhand Autism Prognosis 61
Appendix 67

1. Introduction

Secondhand Autism Defined

Autism is figured to occur with a frequency of 1 in 88 children. The rate during the early 1990's was 19 in 10,000; putting today's rate in 1990's numbers it would be roughly 113 children in 10,000 diagnosed with autism. There is debate over the reasons for the increased instances of autism, whether it is heightened awareness, altered diagnostic criteria or some unknown variable it doesn't matter; the frequency is up. Within the Autism Spectrum Disorder (ASD) there are five classifications: Autistic disorder, Rett syndrome, Asperger's syndrome, Childhood Disintegrative Disorder and Pervasive Developmental Disorder, Not Otherwise Specified (PDD-NOS). When a child is diagnosed with ASD all members of the family are affected. Although autism is unique to an individual its effects reach parents and siblings without prejudice, much like secondhand smoke from a cigarette affects anyone within breathing range.

Obviously there is a difference between autism and smoking a cigarette. There are a great many differences, but the secondhand effect is the same. My brother John and I spent a lot of time with one of our uncles when we were young. Our uncle often worked in the evening so he was around during the day over summer vacation. He smoked a lot. There was no way for him to smoke a cigarette around us without us breathing in the smoke from his cigarettes. The connection I make when using *secondhand* to refer to autism is that the influence of autism is just as pervasive on the family members, or anyone who lives with a person diagnosed as autistic, as that of tobacco smoke on anyone in close proximity to a smoker. The comparison does not include *any* exposure to an autistic, only intimate exposure such as would occur in a living situation with parents, siblings, extended family or legal guardians.

Though my childhood exposure to secondhand smoke was limited to time spent with my uncle, my case of secondhand autism is embedded in every aspect of my life from the time my brother, Scott, was diagnosed through today. In some ways my secondhand exposure is limited now that I no longer live in the same house as Scott, but he is, and always will be, my brother, and I his. I love Scott and while his autism takes up a lot of my thought towards him, it isn't everything he is. I struggle with autism because on one hand it represents my brother and has provided ample growth experience for my family, but on the other hand it is, in my opinion, a terrible disorder that I wish never existed. Secondhand autism, as a phrase, incorporates the negative connotations of secondhand smoke with my struggle in relating to autism and represents my experience, personal and observed, with what autism does to the family members of the individual with the diagnosis.

What it comes right down to is that, to me, autism is a disease. Some people celebrate the differences autism brings, but I have primarily experienced the frustration, and I am not embarrassed to say I wish autism did not exist. For those who celebrate the diversity of autism, I hope my cynicism does not offend you. This is my experience and understanding of a major influencing aspect of my life, through my own lens of perspective, presented as such. However, in contemplation of the effect autism has had on my family and on me, both positive and negative, I realize that life experiences depend intensely on the meaning we apply to them. Secondhand autism, just like autism itself, is a unique condition, sometimes at odds with itself.

Autism Defined

Word origins are often very helpful in understanding and remembering the definition of a word. Autism has for its root the Greek *autos* and *ismos*, which means self and "state of being," respectively (Autism Epicenter, 2013). Essentially, autism means that the person's focus of relation is to self, not to other people. An autistic child seems to exist outside of the existence of other people, much of the time. He does not seek out friendship with peers, or depending on the severity of disorder, might try to, but have extreme difficulty in doing so. Even relationships with parents are cold or non-existent. Other symptoms contribute to the social isolation that is captured in the name autism and readily observable in those diagnosed with the disorder. Historically, autism was first used to describe an aspect of schizophrenia in the early twentieth century, by psychiatrist Eugen Bleuler, and continued to be associated with schizophrenia into the 1960's (WebMD.com, 2012). Dr. Leo Kanner began using the term in 1943 referring to children he observed who behaved in ritualistic and socially isolated ways (Autism Epicenter, 2013). The ASD diagnoses prevalent today are similar to Kanner's conception of autism.

If autism is widely unfamiliar to people today, it was virtually unknown during Kanner's time. When he began blaming the occurrence of autism on the behavior of the child's mother, as erroneous as the claim is, people believed it. Kanner used the term "refrigerator mother" in saying that mothers whose emotional connection with a child was cold led to the autistic condition; Bruno Bettleheim followed Kanner's writings with contributions of his own supporting the case for parental neglect leading to autism (Laidler, 2004). As is often pointed out, the theory that parental neglect causes autism doesn't hold much water when considering that parents of autistic children often have other children who are not autistic. If the parents are the cause then all of their children (or at least most of them) should be autistic, which isn't the case. It is hard to understand how professionals in the field were able to draw such conclusions, but that is with the information available today, looking through a modern lens. Though their hypothesis has been discredited, Kanner, Bettleheim and many others were pioneers in research and classification of autism and their efforts were foundational to the understanding of autism held today.

Autism is more prevalent in boys than in girls. As there is still no known cause of autism, no one knows why there is a difference based on gender. Some people believe autism is the result of external factors only; that it is caused by allergy or poor nutrition, or even childhood vaccinations. According to the CDC (Centers for Disease Control and Prevention) there are no known links between vaccinations and cases of autism (CDC, 2012). Many parents still fear vaccinations as a possible cause of autism. Though evidence doesn't exist to prove a causal link between vaccination and autism, there is no evidence to say that there is absolutely no link at all. It may be the case that autism occurs when a genetic factor meets an external trigger, such as a vaccination, for whatever reason, or a food allergy, or environmental toxins. Unfortunately it simply isn't known yet. With increasing instances of ASD diagnosis the public's awareness of the disorder rises, and, of course, money for research follows public attention.

Autism is marked by deficiencies in communication, social interaction, sensory perception, adherence to routine and perseveration. Clinically, it is a developmental disorder. As previously mentioned, diagnoses fall on a spectrum. Because of the spectrum designation, no two autism diagnoses are the same. On one end you have the "classic" autism, autistic disorder, which is categorized by little-to-no verbal communication and pronounced self-stimulating (stimming) behaviors, while on the other end you have an individual that some would classify as simply being "awkward" or "quirky." Being called a spectrum disorder is a double-edge sword for autism research. With the spectrum, more children are being diagnosed with autism than otherwise would be, which brings more attention to the disorder, hopefully opening up new research endeavors and more effective therapies. This is good, but on the flip-side you have a more watered-down version of autism, effectually spreading attention out among the many children diagnosed, drawing attention away from the extreme cases. If what is now called "classic" autism has different causation than the higher functioning forms of the disorder, then the spectrum classification might prevent focused research on all aspects of the disorder. Diagnostics and theories of causation can be controversial topics of discussion in relation to autism.

Specifically, communication is deficient in verbal and written forms. Echolalia is a term used to describe a common practice of autistics. When asked a question, or greeted, the autistic individual will repeat what has been said, rather than formulate an appropriate response. Some autistics are able to maintain a working set of phrases and terms, but are not able to generate statements of intent or desire, or express feelings. Typically, phrases will lack appropriate propositions and conjunctions, among other literary and grammatical expectations. Literacy is not out of the question for autistics, though it is severely delayed and limited in most cases. For some, written communication is not as limited as verbal communication. Due to motor impairments some individuals are able to communicate through typing even better than handwriting. Facilitated Communication (FC) is a common practice with autistics, wherein a trained therapist aides an individual in controlling hand movement in typing, though the therapy is viewed skeptically by many parents and professionals.

Social skills are delayed, skewed or non-existent with autism. Cues such as head nodding or finger pointing are common supplements to verbal communication, but are likely to be completely missed by autistics. Social referencing, common among young children to know how to react in a given situation, is mostly absent with autism. Rather than make eye contact, autistics will typically watch the mouth of a person speaking to them. The body language that we use to help get our message across in a conversation is typically not perceptible by autistics. Because of sensory perception differences, hugging and hand shaking might be unwelcomed by the autistic person, let alone the fact that the interactive social significance of such behaviors might not be understood.

All people perceive their surroundings differently. Perception is based on biology as well as experience. Perception is the processing which occurs in the brain after stimulus is received by sensory organs. Damaged sense organs are not part of the autism diagnosis, though faulty perception is. This means that while the eyes, ears, nose, tongue and skin work in receiving signals, something in the brain differs from most people in regards to processing the information. For some autistics, a whisper sounds like a shout, a gentle hum of electricity in a light fixture might sound like a jet engine rumble, a dim light might seem like the brightness of the sun, a soft blanket might feel as coarse as sandpaper, and so on. This aspect of autism might be the most difficult to appreciate. It seems easier to understand how there can be communication deficiencies and under developed social cues than to understand sensory perceptive differences. These differences are why some autistics constantly wear ear muffs to block sound or only a certain type of clothing or fabric because of how it feels.

Perseveration is a process of repeating or focusing on one thought, phrase or behavior. Some autistic children perseverate on specific cartoons, others fixate on a toy or game. Adherence to routine is also prevalent with autism. An autistic child might stay with a very strict routine for long periods of time, wherein the same clothes are worn, the same food is eaten and the same activities carried out. Interruptions to the routine result in obvious displeasure, possibly in the form of screaming, crying or physical tantrums.

While autism can be filtered down to a few key phrases, and is done so with the diagnostic criteria to a degree, it is a vast disorder. Autism is frustrating, never-ending and invasive. It never sleeps (literally, with some individuals) and doesn't go on vacation (sometimes it prevents the family from doing so). Its cause is unknown and it is incurable. In its most severe manifestations it can seem like a prison sentence. However, to the committed family member, though never easy, the process of caring for an autistic child or sibling can be rewarding in the way that it teaches compassion, charity and patience.

It is widely agreed that even though there is no cure for autism, early detection leading to early treatment yields the best results as far as helping a child overcome some or all of the developmental delays. Autistic disorder is only diagnosed before age three; any time after that age will likely pull a diagnosis of one of the other syndromes or disorders in the spectrum (WebMD, 2012). The symptoms will include verbal communication deficiencies or delays, social isolation including avoidance of peer interaction, hyper-focus on objects or themes, strict preference for routine and repetitive behaviors or audible expressions (Autism Society, n.d.). Unusual reaction to sensory stimulation is also a hallmark of autistic disorders. While expression of one or more of these symptoms doesn't indicate the existence of autism in a child, they should be noted as red flags. There are countless sources of information about autism diagnosis and therapy available online. Read everything you can and find the common ground. Even in autism research and information sharing there are biases and extremes that can generate misinformation. Autism is different in every child, though symptoms are the same. What works for one child in improving communication or helping to alleviate repetitive behavior may not work for another. Stick to the .org and .edu websites, or reputable .com's, and, most importantly, speak to your child's physician or a psychologist.

This book in no way attempts to provide diagnostic criteria or extensive information about autism in all cases. I will relate the experiences of my family and share what I believe to be some common factors of autism. The purpose of this book is to provide a window into one family's experience with autism and to give attention to the side effects of autism, that is, what happens to the rest of the family when a child is diagnosed. Your experiences or those of your friends, cousins, nephews, aunts and whoever may be similar. Everyone experiences autism differently and to each his or her own experience deserves respect.

2. Autism in my family

This section represents what I remember, but only in brief form. Because I experienced my life as it was happening, and having no other experience to compare to, it is difficult to think of all of the abnormalities that accompany life with autism. I hope that in the near future my parents will undertake to write out the full story of autism in our family. I have read some notes my mom has written which has helped me understand autism from her perspective much better. For the purposes of this book I am going to keep this section short (relatively speaking) and incorporate more of our experiences in the following sections.

Scott was just about three years old when my parents first took him to a doctor with questions about his development. He was on track for the standard age-graded stages of development – crawling, walking, talking, etc. – until he seemed to regress, starting between 18 and 24 months. Scott is the fourth of my parents' six children: Laura (33), me (31), John (29), Scott (25), Alison (23) and Shannon (14) [ages current at time of publication]. Alison was born right around the time when Scott's abnormal behavior started making my parents worry.

Initially Scott's change in development was thought to be a reaction to Alison's birth. My mom recalls:

> *About this time Scott stopped making eye contact. He no longer responded to his name. He'd walk right past us as though we were not there. He lost his ability to engage in imaginative play. He lost the few words he once used. He would spin himself or objects, wiggle his fingers in front of his eyes, repeatedly drop toys to watch them fall, put his face right against the TV screen and squint up his eyes, watch the same one or two videos over and over (fast forwarding and rewinding them at certain spots), hold books up very close to his face and do the same squinting thing. If we interrupted what he was doing or disrupted his routine, he would scream and cry. He slept only 2-3 hours at night. Scott showed absolutely no interest in toilet training (personal communication with Janet Brodie, 2009).*

As Scott wasn't the first child, all of these behaviors stood out as different from my parents' older children. They started to compare Scott's behavior with what they had seen years earlier in a home for adult men with disorders that prevented them from living on their own. They used to go to the home with a friend as volunteers in order to help out at parties and events. By the time he was three my parents decided it was time to seek a doctor's opinion on Scott's development.

The neurologist who initially observed Scott gave my parents the nomenclature for Pervasive Developmental Disorder – Not Otherwise Specified (PDD-NOS). They had no idea what this meant beyond the portion of the title that makes sense, *developmental disorder*. This meant that Scott wouldn't develop on the same track as the average child. Well, not quite as succinct as that. Two years later a second neurologist was consulted and this time after considerable observation and interaction the doctor said autism.

Through lots of research at the library, Mom had become familiar with autism since the first diagnosis, and wasn't surprised by the second diagnosis.

Dad borrowed a book from a friend which was essentially a catalog of testimonials from parents whose children had disabilities. Sections of this book, twenty three years later, are still emblazoned in my parents' memories. Mom remembers one writer saying that having a sick child is a strain on a marriage, and having a child with a disability is like having a sick child all of the time.

Researching autism in 1990 was a lot different than researching autism in 2013; for one thing it was still several years before access to the Internet would become common place in the home through 56k dial-up modems. Mom had to go to the library and make photocopies or check out books. Either that or go to a book store in hopes of finding a relevant book on the shelf, there was no Amazon.com. It wasn't simply access to information that made research difficult; the information just wasn't as available as it is today. Autism wasn't as commonly diagnosed twenty years ago. Diagnostic criteria have changed since then, but awareness of autism has also increased. Autism probably doesn't occur more frequently today than it did twenty years ago, but it seems like it does because of the attention it receives and because of the inclusion of several disorders into the spectrum. Today it is easy to find information about autism simply by typing the term into an internet search engine. Autism even gets regular mention in television news programs and commercials. But in 1990 you either knew what autism was or you didn't, and if you didn't it took a lot of effort to learn.

Unfortunately, being a scholar regarding autism still doesn't change things when your child is diagnosed. The information my parents gathered helped them realize that there were other children who were autistic and other parents who were familiar with what they were now experiencing. They also learned about countless forms of therapy and teaching methods. Our family had a goal of helping Scott recover from autism, something that was reported in various cases written in books, and even a made for TV movie. Autism could be defeated. We know now that some forms or cases of autism, or perhaps autistic traits, can be defeated, but not all of them. What followed the education period for my parents was the treatment period, which lasted the better part of the last twenty years, before they realized Scott's form of autism *is what it is*; while still worth the effort to help Scott achieve progress wherever possible, for the most part his development is halted. But this realization didn't come until after the applied behavioral analysis (ABA) methods, acupuncture, reflexology, kinesiology, Reiki (stress reduction therapy – Japanese origin), craniosacral therapy, horseback riding therapy, auditory integration therapy, sensory integration theory, prescription medication, special diets, vitamins, specialized school, picture boards, assistive electronic devices and facilitated communication, to name a few.

We didn't want to change Scott, we simply wanted to be able to communicate with him and know what he felt. We wanted to know what he needed and wanted in order to feel comfortable and happy. We wanted to know why he was crying or why he bit his hand to the point of permanent scarring. We wanted to know if he was comfortable and happy. Wanting to know but not being able to find out is one of the hallmarks of secondhand autism. The parents, the siblings – all caregivers – constantly want to know, but no matter how they ask, no matter how we ask Scott, there is usually no answer. There are plenty of questions, but very few complete answers.

Scott displayed the stereotypical behaviors of autistic disorder. He followed patterns and routines. For years he would line up a random assortment of action figures and cereal box toys, always in the same order, but no obvious purpose such as shortest to tallest or grouped by like colors. It was a random line up that he repeated every time. He would line up candy too, and whatever else he had. The candy would actually be grouped by color, fruit snacks included, before he ate them.

Scott has a focus on letters and words. The letter perseveration (jargon meaning hyper focus on an object or theme) began when he was two or three. One day he used some letter tiles from a board game to spell short words he had seen on a cartoon. Mom bought him some building block style letter tiles. He used these to spell words from the cartoons at first, but then evolved into spelling out the credits for whatever he was watching, for example, all of the animators who worked on the movie. Mom was able to teach Scott the alphabet, how to say the letters as well as write them, but he preferred to dictate rather than write for himself. When he was about seven there was a list of over 100 names – animators, producers, directors, etc. – that he would dictate to mom every day in the same order. In some cases he would misspell a name, have her erase what she wrote, and then spell it correctly. It was all part of the routine.

When we lived in New Jersey there was a specialized school for autistic children, 50 miles away in Neptune, NJ. Scott attended there until we moved to Vermont in 1995. It was difficult for Mom to put Scott on a bus for the hour plus drive, one way, to the school each day, but she felt it was the best option for him. Not being able to talk to Scott about his experiences and what he did at the school, how he felt about it, was the worst part. After moving to Vermont, Scott was home schooled, but the school district wouldn't provide any assistance that way. They operated under inclusion, which put Scott in a normal classroom with a behavioral interventionist. I don't want to demean the position (behavioral interventionist), but the requirement is a high school diploma and the willingness to restrain an over active child if necessary. I've been through a job interview for such a position myself; I didn't take the job. My parents were hopeful to have people working with Scott who knew autism and had extensive training in forms of therapy. Sadly this hope wasn't always realized, but where experience with autism was lacking, usually a kind heart took its place. We have had some absolutely wonderful people help Scott and be his friend over the years. Schooling hasn't always turned out ideally, but many of the people involved with Scott have been great.

The school, in conjunction with the County mental health agency, focused primarily on the method of facilitated communication (FC) for working with Scott's communication abilities. FC is a controversial pseudo-scientific approach to communication therapy. The American Psychological Association denounced it as a viable form of therapy, and subsequent peer reviewed journals have published studies debunking the FC methods (Wegner, Fuller & Sparrow, 2003). In the face of this evidence the County continues to champion FC. Scott has participated in the FC program for about 13 years. My parents haven't seen the improvements that FC promoters claimed could occur. In my dad's words, all the various care providers and school personnel have done is to "mind him."

Over the years Scott has developed a little bit in his verbal communication, but his ability to reason is still under developed or non-existent. He communicates in fragmented sentences, usually with independent phrases and words. Echolalia (jargon for repeating the words and phrases heard, most children phase through this, but outgrow it) is common, repeating the question he is asked, or if given two suggestions to choose between he'll repeat the last suggestion and say "yes." He'll let someone know when he is hungry, and what he wants to eat, simply by saying the type of food, or "kitchen, please." The kitchen at our parents' house, along with every other room, door and window, is locked down, either to keep Scott in or keep him out. On several occasions he has gotten out of the house through a window or unlocked door. Luckily he has always been found and brought home safely, but the fear we all experience in the time he is missing is terrible.

On one of those occasions of escape, Scott made it into a neighbor's homes, likely looking for candy. He has also made the mile walk to a small grocery store in our neighborhood. One time he was picked up on a freezing cold day by a police officer who spotted him pulling mail out of mailboxes. Scott likes to scan the grocery store advertisements and circle the items he likes. We assume this was what he was looking for in the mailboxes. The police officer was familiar with autism and recognized something of that nature in Scott. He brought Scott to the emergency room where they were able to look up Mom's phone number after Scott was able to answer their question "what's your name?" We are grateful to the police officer who helped Scott that day. Incidentally, this has been the only time Scott was picked up by the police, although he has developed minor notoriety as a shoplifter. On more than one occasion, with our family or with community support workers, Scott has been known to pull a previously unnoticed candy bar out of a pocket or his bag well after a visit to the store. I can't give any more details, for one because I don't have any, but two, I'm not sure what the statute of limitations is on shoplifting.

So the kitchen is locked, and he'll seek help to get in when he is hungry. Other common phrases he uses are "bubble bath, towel, please" and "I need to go to [McDonalds, Walmart, store, etc.]." When he was still in school a common one was "no school today." Actually, he still says that one. He knows my name, but occasionally when he asks for something from me he'll use the static phrases, such as "pizza please mommy." He knows I'm not Mom, but I think the words are more packaged phrases than individually defined.

Overall his communication is as basic as it gets. He does understand what we say more than the limited messages he communicates to us, but he doesn't reason as much as he responds to directions. We can communicate immediate needs with him, in general, but anything deeper – wishes, dreams, goals, experiences, perceptions – is impossible.

Locking doors and rooms extended beyond Scott's safety. Any possessions that the rest of us wanted to keep in working order had to be hidden or locked up. A bag of candy left where Scott could get it was as good as gone. Depending on what type of behavioral phases Scott was passing through, books and paper goods wouldn't be safe if exposed. He would rip them up or write on them. Clothes were even a target for a while. Scott would collect all of the clothes he could, his own or anyone else's, and put them all on. It wasn't uncommon to find him with a dozen pairs of pants layered on. This, we assume, has to do with the sensation of pressure on his body, which is a common method of stimulation with autistic disorders. We had to keep everything locked up if we didn't want Scott to get it. I've compared our home experience to that of a correctional officer with a ring of keys, locking and unlocking doors everywhere he goes. I still have a set of house keys though I no longer live there. On the ring are keys for the front door, back door, laundry/utility room, kitchen and two bedrooms. Without those keys I can watch TV in the living room or use the bathroom, everything else is locked up.

Autism turned a lot of non-consumables into consumables. I've worn out clothes, but it takes years in some cases. Scott occasionally rips up his clothes, even shoes sometimes. Blankets, pillows and mattresses should all last a long time, but not with Scott. He shreds mattresses apart and "unstuffs" pillows. VCR machines and cassettes lasted months at best. The transition to DVDs wasn't very much help. DVD players might have lasted a little longer than

VCRs, but the disks themselves are too delicate for his treatment of them. Scott likes to watch movies on fast forward or in rewind. The machines can't handle the frequent switching between modes. He now has an iPad and watches cartoons on YouTube, I don't think he can do the fast forward and rewind watching on there, but he seems content with it. Even flooring and walls have become consumables. The house we moved into in Vermont was carpeted, except for the kitchen, bathrooms and utility room. Over the years the carpeting was all removed. Scott's toilet training was a long process. Even after he was using the toilet on his own there were times when he simply wouldn't. Without getting into the specifics of it, that takes a toll on a carpet and makes a good argument for having tiled floors. Incidentally my dad's skill at floor installations has improved over the years. Currently, Scott is not allowed to have any writing tools, otherwise his list of what he wants for Christmas gets written across the walls, as exists along the hallway and in the dining room right now.

Happily, Scott isn't self-injurious, aside from biting his hand, which he seemed to do out of frustration most of the time, but occasionally he just seemed to be doing it for the stimulation (in the jargon this is known as "stimming"). There is a constant concern for his safety, however. If you don't know where he is then he could be anywhere. All outside doors are dead bolted, needing a key to get in or out. Windows that aren't behind locked doors in bedrooms have angle brackets to prevent them from opening wide enough for Scott to climb out of, something that has gotten more difficult for him as he got bigger. Initially the refrigerator and a few cabinets in the kitchen had locks on them in order to control food consumption or keep from messes being created, but once Scott went through a phase of using steak knives to scratch his itching feet, the whole kitchen was locked up. In my parent's house this meant building a wall around an open kitchen layout. One time my parents were woken up by the dog barking when a t-shirt Scott had thrown over a lamp began smoldering and filling his bedroom with smoke. Another time a foam earplug he wears because of his sensitivity to noise became lodged deep inside his ear canal. He found a pair of scissors and brought them to Mom and said "Ear hurt. Cut it out." "Cut it out" is a common phrase for Scott, that's what he says for us to cut up his food for him. I suppose the practice of cutting up his pizza or waffles stems from when he was little and it was easier for him to eat that way. Now it is all part of the routine. The phrase "cut it out" has evolved though, at least for Scott.

He is able to feed himself, although food preparation needs to be done under supervision or by someone else, even pouring milk for cold cereal. He dresses himself, bathes himself and uses the toilet on his own, but again, these are on a basic level. The point is that between his communication ability and the tasks of daily life, Scott requires constant assistance and attention. Dad shaves Scott with an electric razor several times a week. He could not be autistic on his own. Our family has all been autistic with him. This is what I mean by secondhand autism.

3. Autism's Effect on Parents

Parent and Child Relationship

I do not have an autistic child. Personally, I hope I never do. I do have parents who have an autistic child. I know that it is one of the most difficult developmental disabilities a child can have. While I don't have an autistic child, my wife and I do have one daughter so far. I know the joy and trepidation that precede the birth of your first child, and likely all children. I remember thinking about how life would change with her birth. How would I change in response to having a child? I remember wondering about her health. My wife and I each have a sibling on the autism spectrum; does this mean our children would be at higher risk than average to have developmental delays? Even when I wasn't thinking about the potential risk of ASD specifically I wondered about our daughter and what she would be like and how she would develop and how great it would be to experience her growth, education and development with her. She is now just under one year old and I can't wait for her to begin talking so we can get to know her even more. I don't like to think about how all that could change if she is autistic.

Considering my experience with my daughter I think the diagnosis of autistic disorder, like my brother, or any of the diagnoses of ASD would be earth shattering in the matter of impaired communication alone. After three healthy, normally developing children my parents experienced the pain of learning that they might not ever get to communicate fully with their son. From my perspective I think this is the most difficult aspect of the relationship between parent and autistic child. Communication is a central aspect of social and family life. Libraries of books exist regarding communication. As a topic it can be majored in at universities around the world. People devote their lives to work revolving around communication. Just try to get through one day without communicating with another person. For most people it likely is impossible. Try not communicating with someone you spend all day with, that would probably be difficult even with great effort. Other disabilities do include communication problems and I don't mean to imply that ASD has the market cornered on this symptom; I simply mean to emphasize the weight of this symptom.

When a baby cries she is telling her parents that she needs something. Often it is food or sleep, or she is uncomfortable from a diaper that needs changing. Crying is a helpful alert, but it doesn't communicate the exact need. Autistic communication is sometimes like this. The child can communicate that they need or want something, but it can be difficult to find out exactly what that need or want is. It can be very frustrating for a parent to try to discuss this with their autistic child at four, nine or even fifteen years of age. The lack of communication ability hinders the parent from knowing how to help their child feel satisfied. It isn't only in the area of needs and wants that a parent longs for knowing what their child is trying to say. Parents want to be able to talk with their children and get to know them. They want to know the child's interests and goals and fears. They want to help the child achieve or overcome these things. With a normal child this can all be accomplished through conversation, with autistics it isn't so easy, or isn't even possible at all.

Personal relationships that don't involve communication can hardly be called relationships, except for in the case of parents whose children have communication disabilities. If you were to consider the factors that define a personal relationship I imagine you would come up with things like physical proximity, shared likes and dislikes, common goals or purposes, similar beliefs and probably the ability to communicate these things between two people. While communication isn't absolutely necessary for a relationship, in social terms it really helps. Parents of autistic children experience one-way communication, often speaking to a child who either seems oblivious to their existence or stares blankly without response.

Recently my dad reported sitting across from Scott at the table in the kitchen while Scott was having breakfast. My dad sat there watching him and then said, "Paul is writing a book. John might be moving to Pennsylvania." Scott never looked up from eating, never made any type of vocal acknowledgement; there was no diversion from what he was doing to signify that he was aware of dad's presence or that he had said anything. People might joke that this is the typical teenager response and then everyone laughs. But Scott is twenty-five, and even if teenagers act like they aren't paying attention, or are overly preoccupied, they do hear and acknowledge things, if only once in a while. I know it hurts my mom when Scott is crying and she asks what's wrong and he doesn't respond. Experience taught her early on to just bear with it when Scott would lie on the floor and cry, non-responsive to all efforts of consoling. If she didn't learn to bear it she never would have made it this long, but to think that she ignores it or isn't affected by Scott's crying, even now, would be a mistake. I know my parents want more than anything to be able to communicate with Scott and know how he is feeling.

Beyond communication the parent/child relationship is severely affected in interactive play. Autistic children tend to play independently. They aren't as quick to engage in social play, or may not participate in it at all. Their play doesn't follow the play of their peer group, either. Where preschool boys may be prone to play with trucks and perhaps set up a construction site in the sand box, an autistic child may be content to spin tops or plates, or repeatedly stack blocks and knock them down, without any story line to their type of play. Scott, for example, would sit in the sandbox and lift handfuls of sand high above his head and then slowly allow the sand to sift through his fingers and fall. He would simply watch the sand. Sometimes he would do this with pebbles or leaves.

Parents can get down on the floor and engage their autistic child in play, but soon the child may seem to shut off and create distance between himself and the parent and engage in individual play. In many cases there is no interest in the age specific toys or television programs. Team sports and heavily choreographed activities may not hold the interest of the child or the child might not be able to grasp the concept and learn the game. Or the child becomes over stimulated and requires removal from the current environment in order to calm down. Parents often have expectations and dreams of sharing their favorite sports, toys and games with their children, only to find, in the case of some autistic children, that what is important to the parent doesn't even warrant recognition from the child.

One of the therapy programs our family tried was to isolate one of us in a dedicated play room with Scott, usually for an hour at a time, and just follow him around and do whatever he was doing. Our parents and each of us older children, along with community volunteers would keep this up for most of the day, every day, for several years. This method had seen success in the case of the therapy creator's child, but we didn't see much improvement in Scott's development. It did provide us each with time to play with Scott, however clinical it may have been. The patterns of play my parents employed with me were different than those they employed with Scott. Everything was always different with Scott.

Autism creates a physical, mental and emotional barrier between parent and child. Sensory differences, either sensitivities or deficiencies, interfere with basic touch for autistic children. They may shy away from affection, such as hugs and kisses, or appear to respond with pain from playful tickling. Some autistic children can't bear even the slightest touch from another person, while simultaneously needing pressure on their body to feel comfortable. This might manifest in wearing multiple layers of clothing (as with Scott), or particularly tight clothing; also, covering up with heavy blankets, pillows or sofa cushions. Even when a child may accept hugs, they might never offer them. Like all aspects of autistic behavior this, too, varies from child to child. It is emotionally draining for a parent to extend affection year after year and rarely, if ever, receive it.

All of these factors contribute to stress in the parent/child relationship. There is no getting away from the fact that autism presents a clear challenge in developing this relationship. However, the difficulties do not mean that the relationship cannot exist or is not worth the effort. Autistic children likely have the same emotional needs as every other child. Unless future research finds specific areas of the brain, where emotional needs occur, to be damaged or non-functioning, we won't know for sure. I know from experience that even though the outward expression of behavior seems aloof most of the time that there is a connection between autistic children and family members. It may be more difficult for parents to constantly give without ever feeling a response, but it is the only way. My mom remembers a quote from a book she read which says something to the effect of having an autistic child is like living underwater: it can't be done, but you have no other choice.

Love is the only way to explain a healthy parent and autistic child relationship. For some parents the demands are too high and they quit or give their child away. Knowing the difficulty of raising an autistic child, though only as a sibling observer, it is difficult to judge parents for quitting, but for the same reason I know that whatever the difficulty is it can be done. It just requires a lot of love, the selfless kind.

My parents have shown me and my siblings what love looks like. Love from a parent to a child looks like sacrificing personal interests, sleep deprivation, never taking even a few minutes to relax, always aware, constantly worrying…always providing. Autistic children require a lot of effort; their parents are always providing, both time and energy. My mom has noted the feelings she has had when seeing normal children, her own and others, achieve accomplishments like good report cards, high school plays, learning to play instruments, high school and college graduations, careers, marriages and parenthood, and then considering how Scott will never experience these things, or at least, not in the same way. Scott has graduated high school, although clearly under different standards. She has hoped for even the slightest improvements in development, only to be frustrated again and again. But she and Dad have never stopped loving Scott and providing for him at their own expense, over and over and over.

Husband and Wife Relationship

Marriage brings some unique challenges. Specifically, a successful marriage requires each partner to give priority to their spouse above their personal interests. After a lifetime of struggling for individual identification and pursuing self-interests, for better and for worse, the individual enters into marriage and becomes part of a team. In order for the team to thrive, each partner needs to sacrifice self in order to bolster the other. When each partner contributes in this manner appropriately, each is lifted to heights neither could ever attain alone. This is foundational for any marriage. Now introduce children and everything changes. Financial matters come along and change things again. There are countless forces and influences that can cause distress in a marriage, and so it takes a strong commitment to keep a marriage alive. It requires work, and once again, it requires love. The force that binds the parent to the child against all difficulty is the same force that binds spouses together against all difficulty: love.

It is commonly rumored that parents with autistic children face an 80% divorce rate. Research by Brian Freedman in 2010 determined that the difference between autistic and non-autistic households, as far as children living with either both biological or both adoptive parents, was practically the same (Kennedy Krieger, 2010). Freedman is clinical director of the Center for Autism and Related Disorders at the Kennedy Krieger Institute in Baltimore. In the same year Hartley, et al. found a higher divorce rate among parents of autistic children (23%) than among parents of non-disabled children (13%), and determined that the risk timeframe for divorce was longer (childhood to about age 30) than for parents of non-disabled children (Hartley, et al., 2010). Statistics or not, autism is a unique and heavy stressor for a married couple. Having any child introduces new patterns of day to day living for a couple. Time once spent pursuing personal interests or time together is now challenged by the needs of the child. When the child has autism the need is even greater. Personal hobbies disappear, as do date nights. A diagnosis of autism absolutely does not mean imminent divorce, but parents should be aware of the new demands on their relationship with each other.

Autism is not an individual disorder; it is shared by the family, granted, the one child bears the brunt of the disorder. The focus in a family with an autistic child becomes the child. Parents now see the child before all else. The child becomes the reason for doing or not doing just about anything. If spouses aren't careful this can lead to justification and rationalization, in other words, autism can become an excuse. But this is worst case scenario and the literature on the topic indicate that marriages that are struggling before diagnosis will likely continue to struggle after diagnosis, however, marriages that are working well before diagnosis may even become stronger after diagnosis. Autism, just like any other dramatic event or situation, causes stress. Stress is both good and bad.

It takes a normal amount of good stress, eustress, to be alive and moving forward, but distress, the bad stress, eats away at health and mood if left unchecked. A marriage that is unstable or partners who are struggling in their relationship might not be able to handle the added stress of autism. The constant coordination necessary to ensure the child's safety in the house as well as appointments with doctors or at school, in addition to whatever therapy that is going on, and providing material needs all works together as a collective responsibility that must be carried. If it isn't carried together it will be carried alone, and that can be enough to drive someone away. One parent might leave the marriage relationship out of fear of the responsibility, or selfishness in not wanting to accept the responsibility. Or a parent might leave the marriage because they are doing everything alone and feelings of animosity grow towards the spouse because they feel the other person isn't contributing enough. In this case the parent providing for the child might not leave the location, but emotionally they leave the relationship. Autism doesn't cause divorce, but it exacerbates existing problems or conditions that might cause it. This isn't the optimal path; parents of autistic children need the companionship and support of marriage, and autistic children need the loving care of both parents, as do all children.

As a student of psychology I have spent considerable time reading research articles and studying statistics and research methods. I am no expert, by any reach, but I have more than a layman's understanding of these things. Statistics can easily be manipulated to tell a story a certain way. As I've considered the so-called rumor of high divorce rates among parents of autistic children, in light of reading about the recent study that says such high divorce rates don't exist, I wonder if there is something else at play. Whenever you consider statistics you want to learn all you can about the method of study and how the data was analyzed. For example, 25 years ago the rates of autism diagnosis was less than it is today. Was that because there were fewer cases, less awareness or tougher diagnostic criteria? We can't know for sure, I suppose, but if the diagnostic criteria changed, then autism didn't increase, rather other disorders became autism. When considering how stats can be used to mislead – intentionally or not – text books often cite the example that the rates of death by heart disease and cancer are so much higher today than in 1900. In 1900 the life expectancy was shorter than in 2000. Many sicknesses and infections that killed people in 1900, before they ever got old enough to develop cancer or heart disease, no longer existed in 2000. If you look at only the instances of heart disease deaths in 1900 and 2000 you might draw a conclusion that something changed in people's diet or lifestyles to cause the increase, something bad, but looking at the broader picture, it might have been something good. People live longer.

The point in considering statistics is that maybe the 80% divorce rate that is commonly repeated was true 20 years ago when autism was what is now classified as autistic disorder. Maybe this more severe branch of ASD did lead to more divorces. Perhaps the numbers have evened out now because of the other disorders grouped into the spectrum that aren't quite as severe. Children with ASD, not autistic disorder, often experience full integration in school and even participate in school athletic programs, earn drivers licenses and hold jobs. Their autistic-like tendencies warrant diagnosis within the autism spectrum, but they can function in society on their own. This isn't to say it is easy for the child or the family, I think the same secondhand autism effect takes place, but it is different and in my opinion not as trying on a marriage. But this is my speculation, tainted by my admitted chip-on-the-shoulder because my experience with autism has been more dramatic by my perception than that of other cases I have heard about. I know it isn't fair to judge others through my personal autobiographical lens, but I do it, and I try not to. With matters of autism it is more difficult for me to not feel bitter. It may be the case that diagnostic changes over the years, opening the range of what autism is defined as, has made a change in the divorce rate statistics. I don't harp on this to support divorce in the case of severe autism, only to emphasize the fact that having an autistic child can be a major cause of distress, and friends, coworkers and school professionals need to be aware of this effect on a marriage and hopefully be sympathetic to it.

My parents will celebrate 35 years of marriage this year, 23 of which were with autism in the family. Husbands and wives can stay together, and stay strong, with autism. Autism changes everything, but it isn't a death sentence. I know my parents didn't get out for many dates, at least not until Laura was old enough to stay home with the rest of us. But even then, dates weren't exactly the same as they might be for the parents without autistic children, often, as I remember it, they only went to the grocery store, but even that was something at the time. It wasn't easy for them to leave us with just anyone. Teenage girls from the neighborhood aren't exactly trained for dealing with autism. Once we were older, having become somewhat of experts in autism, at least Scott's brand of it, we made good babysitters for ourselves. By the time we were competent watchers for staying home without our parents it had already been a lot of years where our parents weren't able to go out together without any children. Driving to the various doctor's offices and therapy locations became the most common experience my parents had for time together. It was often just them and Scott, and as my mom recalls, since Scott wasn't communicative, she and my dad were able to talk and have some semblance of privacy together.

Not having time alone together can be damaging to a relationship. Our parents really never had any time alone together. With six kids that would be hard enough, but incorporate autism and it's nearly impossible. Scott's sleep patterns weren't the same as the rest of us in the house. He was up at night a lot, and between the noise he'd make and the general worry that accompanies autism, so were our parents. I've heard of soldiers returning from war who suffer from states of hyper vigilance, meaning that they are constantly aware of what is going on and suspicious of every little stimulus, as a possible threat. In our home, autism was a constant battle and there was a need for constant awareness of where Scott was and what he was doing. The hyper vigilance that develops within the home in response to autism is a constant symptom of secondhand autism. When mom wasn't awake at night with exhaustion and feelings of not knowing what to do for Scott, she was constantly being woken up by his noises and her concern.

Hyper vigilance affects the marriage relationship because it makes it difficult for parents to get out of the house even when the child is provided for. New parents leaving their infant child for the first time know something of what this anxiety feels like. The concern for what the child is doing is present, even when the child is not. Sometimes when Scott was out of the house we would hear something and look for him, or ask someone where he was, just to be reminded that he wasn't home at all. This awareness is good because it helps prevent bad situations that might arise, but it is bad because it can make it even more difficult to be alone with your spouse. Marriage needs intimacy, or closeness. Constant worry over one child can interfere with this closeness. It is necessary for each partner to work towards securing time for each other, and not just being together in physical proximity, but together in emotion and attention as well.

Life isn't fair, at least not in terms of fairness meaning equality. My mom has considered the idea of fairness quite a bit in regards to Scott, autism and the rest of our family. She decided that fairness isn't equality, but rather giving to each what is needed. To be fair, Scott needed more than his siblings. Mom did the best she could, but there was always way more than she and my dad could do to meet all of the needs that were there. Autism isn't fair.

Parents want to provide for all of their children's needs. Autistic children have a lot of demanding needs. Autistic children also can be louder in the demand because of their behavior. By louder I mean they do things that draw more attention. This could be hours of repeating the same non-sense words or sounds over and over, or unexplained laughter or crying. Repetitive behaviors repeated for long periods of time such as jumping, rocking or hand waving. Many of the symptoms of autism are loud in this way; they draw attention. I think it becomes easier as time goes on for a parent to lose track of the non-autistic siblings. This isn't to say they aren't involved or become neglectful, but they miss some of the more subtle signs that in other homes would attract attention. Parents who are aware of this possibility, but aren't able to reconcile it may experience increased feelings of guilt or hopelessness.

It depends on the nature of the parent, but for mine it was difficult for them to take Scott to public events because of the negative attention he attracted. My mom couldn't take the constant accusatory remarks and questions from people in stores, on the street and even in church. In the 1990's autism wasn't as prevalent or popular as it is today; it seemed that most people didn't understand it at all. One of my grandmothers believed the theories of Kanner and Beetleheim, placing blame for autism on the parenting style of the mother, in this case, my mother. Because of this ignorance at large and the comments my parents would hear when they took Scott out, along with the difficulty of keeping track of him in a location where he was apt to run away and become lost, my parents didn't take Scott out of the house much (meaning into public where many people would be). This was also the result of wanting to help Scott be comfortable. He still moves a lot and makes noises. He doesn't do well with sitting still and being quiet for hours at a time. To bring him to an elementary school band concert or a high school play or even church seems like it wouldn't be comfortable to Scott. My parents would take turns going to these types of events so that one of them could stay home with Scott. Some events, such as my sisters' drama and music performances often played for several nights, making it possible for each parent to attend, but separately. I suppose in some regards it was as though our parents were divorced when they couldn't both attend different events for us. But I never thought of it that way.

The demands of autism draw away the time and attention parents can give to their other children. I never felt neglected, however. The relationship between parent and non-autistic child in the presence of an autistic child is affected, but likely the difference is more aware to the parent. As a result of the time devoted to Scott, the rest of us, of necessity, adapted to more personal responsibility in taking care of our laundry, feeding ourselves and keeping ourselves entertained, all at a younger age than may have been the case without autism in our family. We didn't know anything different. We knew that our parents loved us and did all they could to provide for us. We knew that Scott's autism made things different in our family from other families, but that just meant things were different, not bad.

The extra stress that exists between husband and wife exists between parent and child as well. It can lead to problems, but doesn't have to. My parents were strengthened in their relationship by their mutual commitment to Scott and each of their children. The relationship between our parents and each of us is strong because of our united commitment to our family. It wasn't always the autism alone, financial difficulty was also a factor, in how our family spent leisure time. We never took long vacations or went very far from home. We didn't go out to eat (other than fast food or ordering pizza take-out), go to movies or visit other family activity centers as a whole family, not often. When we did these things Mom or Dad was typically home with Scott while everyone else went. Autism did affect how our parents interacted with their non-autistic children, but it was the things we could do, such as going for walks around the neighborhood, going to the elementary school playground or walking along the canal tow paths in Princeton, NJ, near where we lived, or simply spending time together at home, that really strengthened our relationships. Our experience has been different than many families in appearance, but certainly not in quality, unless for the better.

4. Autism's Effect on Siblings

Although this whole book is subjective in presentation and concept, this chapter becomes even more so through my heavy reliance on personal experience and the fact that every person is so uniquely different, even between siblings within the same family. In my study of psychology I have spent a lot of time contemplating the debate over which has the strongest influence in the development of a personality: nature or nurture? In much of science there is a tendency to avoid absolute statements using 'never' or 'always.' I think this is a good general rule. To say that nature, meaning genetics, is solely responsible for shaping a life, or the contrary, that nurture, meaning environment, is absolute, is dangerous. For one, we haven't yet figured out a way to know for sure just what is transmitted genetically in terms of personality. We don't even know what is specifically transmitted genetically in autism. Secondly, putting all responsibility on either environment or genetics creates a tendency to blame and shift personal responsibility away from self. The purpose of this philosophical detour is to say that it is a mixture of nature and nurture that shapes a person. Even within the same genetic pool (a blood-family) and the same environment (the home), each individual has a different experience. Our experiences make my siblings and I more like each other than any other people, but we are still vastly different. Our experiences with autism have differed and will be different than any other sibling of an autistic person, but there will be many core similarities as well.

The first thing to consider in the impact of autism on non-autistic siblings is birth order, or at least, the sibling's status of older or younger. As autism is expressed early in childhood, prior to three for autistic disorder and up to a few years later for other ASD classifications, older non-autistic siblings might not be very much older. It all depends on the family, however, so there are no general rules about the likelihood of siblings being this much older or that much younger. The point is that for older siblings there might not be a significant time of life lived without autism in the family, at least not that they will consciously remember later in life; however, the years of birth to age five – viewed by many as the most important years for development – may be drastically affected. Even though autism might not be introduced to the child until they are beginning elementary school they still essentially grow up with it.

I am six and a half years older than Scott, which puts me at about nine years old when he first began expressing autistic symptoms. I remember the process of learning about autism, but only summarily, being still very young at the time. From then on it was a learning process along with the rest of my family. We learned as we lived, each of us becoming an expert in this one instance of autism. I had an older sister and a younger brother when Scott was born. I had play companions that could communicate with me and engage in creative play with action figures and whatever else. I had a brother who could play Nintendo with me and fight with me. We built forts in the yard and played baseball together. I have tried to do these things with Scott, and while we were able to play together and give some semblance of sameness to these activities, they weren't the same.

Playing with an autistic sibling is possible, but it isn't the same as a non-autistic sibling. Baseball wasn't so much baseball with Scott as it was him holding a bat and me trying to toss a ball timing it to his bat speed so the ball would hit the bat. Action figures didn't engage in combat scenarios, they would be lined up. Playing with Scott usually meant jumping or following him around and doing what he was doing, something we picked up from an ABA style therapy program. The sibling relationship still exists, only it exists differently. Once again, there is only one-way communication, and at times the sibling may feel more like an object to be acted upon by the autistic brother than a friend to be played with. But the bond of brother- and sisterhood is not diminished.

We have two sisters who are younger than Scott. Mom recounts that one time when she asked a young Alison what she wanted for her birthday she replied that she wanted Scott to play with her. The brother/sister bond existed among stress and strain. The natural tendency of a child is to interact and play; autism can stress that for the siblings. Happily, children are also naturally compassionate and full of love and understanding. At the time of the birthday request, Scott's play with Alison involved him pushing her and saying "go, Alison" to which she would respond by running while he chased, and they would run in circles around the room. She wanted a more social interactive form of playing, but she always played his games his way.

Alison has been as good a sister to Scott as I can possibly imagine. Her experience with Scott has been, in my opinion, the most demanding. She was born right around the time of Scott's first diagnosis. She grew up immersed in autism. If any of our siblings' attention from Mom and Dad was reduced because Scott absorbed more of it, it was Alison's. Laura, John and I were older and had each other to play with, being relatively close in age and with a few years between us and Scott, but Alison was seven years younger than John and didn't have a close (age-wise) sibling to play with. For her, there is no life without the influence of autism. [Shannon has also lived her entire life with autism, which clearly is inescapable, but I think for her Scott had hit a plateau and didn't absorb as much attention from mom and dad as had been the case when Alison was younger.] Alison spent the most time of any of us attending the same school as Scott. This presented social experiences that are unique to her within our family.

Alison has told me that school with Scott presented some challenges for her personally. She didn't see Scott at school very often, but when she did he was usually looking down and waving his arms and fingers as he typically does. He wouldn't even notice when she'd pass him and say hello. Her friends who knew Scott would say hi to him and tell her when they saw him, but other kids would just stare at him. The aides assigned to him didn't seem very helpful as they walked slowly down the hall or talked with someone while Scott charged down the hallway. Alison never witnessed the aides yelling at Scott, but she did see them yelling at other children labeled for special education. Overall, Alison thought Scott always looked unhappy and agitated at school. I guess even autism can't stop that from happening to a teenager.

The relationship between Alison and Scott is different and can be frustrating, but even without communication there is a sense of reciprocity. I think that reciprocity exists between Scott and each of us. One bit of evidence I find is during a phase a few years ago when Scott was compulsively putting his foot on things. It became something he would need to do before leaving the house. He'd just tap the toe of his shoe on things: the dog's kennel, chairs, the table, the TV, the door, the dog himself. It was impressive the reach Scott had with his feet. Occasionally he would attempt to put his foot on people as well, such as the respite workers (people hired by my parents, funded by the County, to take Scott into the community for a few hours each day, providing a break for my parents and some activity for Scott). Scott never tried to put his foot on our family members during this phase of compulsion. For all of our wondering what is going on in his mind and how he sees us and relates to us, I know that he knew we were his family. The dog, though he lives in the house, wasn't part of the family, he got touched by the foot, but our family weren't treated like objects. Autism does frustrate me, but it isn't how I view Scott. I know the same is true with all of our siblings, and obviously with our parents.

Scott knows we are his family and though he can't or doesn't communicate that in speech or action, he feels it. When Alison asked for the opportunity to play, I suppose in a "normal" fashion, with Scott for her birthday, she didn't get it, but she has had, and has taken, every opportunity to interact with and play with Scott in autism's abnormal way. And Scott is aware of it. We can only offer anecdotal evidence of his awareness and feelings, but that is sufficient. Though the moments don't come unsolicited very often, Scott does express affection. When Mom told me about Alison's request, she also told me that recently, as Alison has been out of state attending university, when Scott was asked what he wanted for his birthday he said "Alison airport airplane." We have wondered whether or not Scott misses his grown up siblings who are out of the house because he misses them or because they were part of his routine. Maybe it is both, we can't know, but I'm sure that even when he can't express it like the rest of us, Scott knows we have a special relationship called family and that is reassuring to me in the moments of frustration.

Having an autistic sibling is like having a super power; as they say, with great power comes great responsibility, only it is reversed: with great responsibility comes great power. Scott's autism has provided constant opportunity for our family to learn patience, selflessness, sacrifice, service, compassion, love, awareness, understanding and countless other welcomed traits and virtues. The increased responsibility we, as siblings, have had to measure up to blessed us with many beneficial qualities. Of course, I think some of the anxieties, worry and hyper vigilance came along as well, but that just balances us out so that our egos don't get out of control. Autism truly has been a thorough teacher. This is part of why I have such a fragmented view of autism. I hate autism because, in my limited perspective, it seems to prevent Scott from having and experiencing things that I think he should get to have; things that I have experienced and am grateful for.

At the same time I am grateful to Scott for living in a dysfunctional body and experiencing life in the manner he does so that the rest of us can be refined and learn so much. I don't think I would be as attentive to other people or to details in life, nor would I be as patient with people (things like computers and machines are another story) if not for my experience with Scott and autism. If I didn't have an eternal perspective (meaning I don't see life ended with mortal death) in regards to life I think that I would be extremely bitter and wish above all else that autism didn't exist and that Scott could have a normal life; however, with an eternal perspective I am humbled that Scott is experiencing autism firsthand, so that we can experience it secondhand and though his progress in life seems halted in so many regards, our family's progress has been expedited. In the New Testament Jesus Christ said that no man has greater love than he who lays down his life for his friends (John 15:13). This can mean, as it often is used to refer to military personnel, someone who offers their life, meaning mortality, in the service of others; but it also means someone who devotes their life, not through death, through living, to the service of others. I don't know how the assignment of disabilities works in the grand plan of life, but whether Scott volunteered or was drafted for this experience, it doesn't matter, he is doing it and when I can think about autism in this manner, rather than the superficial expressions of it, I find peace.

Secondhand Autism

We love Scott. Having an autistic sibling is difficult because sometimes you have to lock things up that you don't want to see destroyed. Sometimes your baseball cards or comic books or video games get destroyed. Sometimes your candy stash gets invaded. Sometimes you can't go as an entire family somewhere because it will be too difficult for Scott or too demanding for mom and dad. Sometimes you can't play with your brother or sister the way you want to. Sometimes you can't recall experiences with that sibling and enjoy times past. But all of these are self-centered, they are not bad, but they focus on the relationship of self to another. What you do have, and it is still difficult, is a change in focus from outward in. Sometimes you have to miss an event to help with the sibling. Sometimes you help prepare food for your brother who can't do it for himself. You do his laundry for him. You clean his room for him. You drive him to the store so he can get a candy bar. You help him brush his teeth. You take him outside and let him throw rocks in the creek, not because it is something you do together, because he is doing his thing and you are just there to watch him and make sure he is safe. You do these things for him, not for yourself. And this is what the relationship is between siblings when one has autism and one does not.

As a teenager I never had a problem telling my parents where I was going or when I'd be back. I was very much used to that type of reporting. We had a changing of the guard mentality about us. If one of the kids was watching Scott we'd give a report when our parents got home. In general we'd often ask each other where Scott was if it had been a while since we'd seen him, even if we weren't specifically tasked with watching him. It was just part of our hyper vigilance and what went on at home. I think this set apart our sibling interactions from other groups of siblings. We were good personnel managers and learned to communicate that type of business between ourselves. With locked doors, and everyone having their own set of keys, but sometimes not all of the necessary keys, we would make sure that whoever was tasked with watching Scott knew where he was and had access to all necessary areas of the house. Essentially, we were Scott's caregivers along with our parents. In a way our sibling role was associated with a co-worker role, and in some ways a parent role.

We engaged in sibling rivalries as younger children, but I don't remember much of that past elementary school for myself. Laura and John and I might have just naturally grown out of it by that point, but that was also the time when Scott was diagnosed with autism. I know the responsibilities that came with caring for our brother accelerated our maturation in some regards; I think one of those ways was in how we related to each other. I'm sure for Alison and Shannon this is what happened. They likely would have matured faster in accountability and responsibility simply because they had significantly older siblings while they were young. Of course, when you are two years, or eleven years, younger than your brother and you pass him in verbal communication and self-maintenance abilities I think that has an effect on you. Shannon and Alison have both experienced what it is like to out develop an older sibling. I see in each of them maturity well beyond their ages.

It is difficult to say how much of our ability to get along was a result of the increased responsibility of caring for Scott, and how much is because of attentive, loving parents. I know that we are united in our care for Scott; that unity has helped us be close to one another, but at the same time, our closeness isn't witnessed in outward expressions of affection. We have a more subdued bond between us. Perhaps it is a little bit of the autism in everyone in our family that causes this. Our family would be close regardless of Scott's diagnosis with autism or not, but I'm certain that autism has been a catalyst for our growth. For all of the difficulty associated with autism in the family, secondhand autism may also take on the meaning of being passed down, such as clothing in a thrift store.

Secondhand Autism

Secondhand isn't only associated with smoking, generating negative connotations, secondhand can also mean extended life. An autistic sibling changes the life of a child, but change can be good as well as bad.

Paul Brodie

5. Notes from My Siblings

It is difficult for me to capture my family's story from everyone's perspective. I have talked with everyone and we've sent e-mails back and forth to collaborate on ideas, but I can't convey the individual voices very well. These are quotes from messages I received that I felt were best presented exactly as I received them, and not interpreted by me.

Shannon (age 14)

I think the first time I really realized there was something wrong with Scott was when I was around 8 years old, when I started having friends over for longer than a few hours. I had to train my friends not to leave valuable things around the house because Scott might get to it or move it somewhere unsafe. I also had to tell them to look the look the other way if Scott was about to take a bath or just got out of a bath because he wouldn't be wearing any clothes. I think one of my friends did end up seeing him right after one of his baths.

They would ask me why our refrigerator had a lock on it and why we kept all the doors locked at all times. I remember always having to ask Mom to open the fridge (before I finally knew how to open the fridge myself) just so I could get a drink or a snack because we also had locks on the cabinets. Before my friends started questioning me, I always thought it was a normal thing to have everything locked at all times, nothing strange.

When Scott got out of the house multiple times, I didn't like how upset Mom got. I guess that's why whenever we went out I would pay close attention to Scott, because I was afraid Mom would be upset if he got away. I remember it being hard for Mom and Dad to plan things because they had to take turns going to school or church events.

When I was younger than 8, I remember being afraid of Scott, not really afraid that he would hurt me or anything like that, he was just different than all of my other brothers and sisters. Scott never calls me by name; he only ever calls me "Baby." I don't mind it, I think it's funny. He calls everyone else by their names, but not me. I guess he only remembers me as a baby and got used to that.

Alison (age 23)

I am never embarrassed at anything anymore since doing theatre; but put me in a store with Scott and my stress hits a peak and I think about it all day and I feel bad for Scott. There's definitely a lot of guilt felt by all of us. We all feel guilty going off with our own lives while Scott just sits at home on an iPad watching movies, but that is what he is comfortable with, that's what he wants to do. Whenever we take him out of the house, Scott gets agitated and asks to go home. Some days he wants to go do something, but most days he wants to stay inside. I took Scott out a lot to restaurants and stores and it was very stressful for me to even be in the car with him because I was afraid he would jump out of the car randomly (which he has done a few times). He always wanted to go to the *Beverage Baron* and he would throw a fit anytime we passed it. I always felt terrible for not stopping, but when I had in the past, he would rush to whatever he wanted (I think he was worried I would take him away before he had time to get what he wanted) and I would try to follow him, but he's so fast and has longer legs than me. So eventually I tried to take different routes because the way he thrashed around in the car made me think he might open the door and just jump out. Maybe that's a ridiculous thought, but I've seen broken glass in the bathroom from when he tried to break out. He scratched up his wrist or hand, I don't remember.

I would get upset that Mom and Dad couldn't go places together. I wanted them to come together when they saw my shows. I know that seems unimportant, but I wanted them to be together when they saw the show. Having them need to come separately made me feel like I wasn't first priority. Every child needs to feel like first priority once in a while, I think. With Scott, every one of us knew he was first priority, and we would never be able to feel like we came first, but you get conditioned to it and I think it makes you a better person in some ways. Hyper vigilant? Yes. Selfless and understanding? Yes.

One time, when the cabinets and refrigerator were locked, before the door came, Scotty seemed agitated and wanted something from the fridge. I walked by and saw so I stopped to open it for him. It was a combination lock that I tended to get wrong at least once before opening it. This was one of those times. Scott suddenly pushed me towards the fridge really hard. I was very startled, but it didn't hurt that much. It must have been during my junior or senior year of high school. I think that was the moment I realized Scott had the temper of a toddler, but the strength of a man and that I needed to be more forceful with him (word-wise, of course). I bellowed at him to sit down and that I would get him something to eat.

I think that if the public school is all we have for a school for Scotty, they should at least get some professionals in there. There are only five or less at a time that need aides at the school. I don't know how they don't have the funding for it. They have funding for sports and theatre productions, but not for my brother to have better communication skills. And if they cannot afford it, they should admit that and say that we should take him somewhere else to get the proper care he needs. People don't seem to care though. They figure since there is no cure, the aides might as well act as babysitters. Although he cannot be cured, he does have the skills to communicate better. I think that anyway. I remember he read a book once to us. A picture book, but he read it all the way through out loud by himself. That went away.

John (age 29)

Having a little brother with severe autism has made me more conscientious and able to understand people better. I say this because I had to learn to communicate with Scott in ways other than normal verbal communication. He has learned a few words in his life that he can speak and sometimes he can express a few thoughts via typing or writing. I never put much thought into it before, but now I can see that Scott communicated a lot to me through body language, eye contact and even past experience.

When I say body language the first thing that comes to mind is how he would get very frustrated and bite his hand and jump up and down as he made different loud noises. He bit his hand so hard that it developed a callus. My parents tried to put lemon juice or other things on his hand to deter him from biting it, but nothing ever worked. He has a pretty disfigured hand because of it. It was always very clear through body language when Scott didn't like something. Ironically he used some of the same body language when he was excited, by jumping up and down and making loud sounds. He would get excited about candy or about going outside to throw rocks in the water.

Eye contact can be rare or empty with autistic children, but I had a few experiences with Scott where we exchanged a few moments of eye contact and he communicated with me through that means. Sometimes it was just him telling me he was frustrated or angry. Other times it was much more spiritual and I felt like he was searching my soul with his gaze. I always felt like I had a special connection with Scott, more so than he had with my other siblings. If he was not autistic then he would have been my little brother who followed me around and tried to do everything I did and we probably would have fought a lot.

When I say past experience I mean just knowing my brother. I knew most of what he liked and didn't like. He didn't like loud noises, or not getting his way, or bugs. He really liked going outside to jump on the trampoline or to throw rocks in the creek by our house. He also liked to go McDonalds to get a Happy Meal or to the store to buy candy. So I knew what he wanted to do most of the time and didn't really need him to communicate. And usually by not protesting something I knew that he was pleased with where we were going or what he was going to do. He was pretty obvious in his discontent.

I also feel that Scott helped me to be a more patient person. That's not to say that I was always patient with him. It was difficult when he would destroy things or put himself into danger. I never had my dog eat my homework, but I did have my brother rip it up or write all over it a few times. Although I say I learned patience from living with Scott, I also cut him a lot of slack since he could not reason or control himself. When I deal with people at work that can reason and could control themselves I am not as patient.

Being a father of two sons now I have thought of what a different life we will have if either ends up being autistic. We have greatly enjoyed watching our toddler learn and grow and develop. To think that all of that development and progression could basically stop and my son could be 2-years-old for his whole life is a sobering thought. It has even influenced our decision to delay vaccinations until our sons are older than 2-years-old. Our pediatrician disagreed with our intentions, but we feel like there is a link to vaccinations and developmental disorders; and if not the cause of autism, at least not worth the risk of SIDS (Sudden Infant Death Syndrome). And that whole debate over autism and vaccinations has been very polarizing and political. Whichever way people believe is the truth they should at least be able to talk about the issue in an open manner.

I also became very sensitive to kids bullying other handicapped kids or using offensive words like "Retard" because of Scott. I would always stand up for other kids that were being picked on. I remember hearing about one bully who had been picking on an autistic kid in my grade during high school. He had turned off the lights when the autistic kid went to the bathroom. At lunch one day the bully was sitting at my table and picking on some of my friends and bragging about tormenting the autistic kid. I told him to stop bullying people or I would have to stop him myself. He didn't like being challenged so he told everyone that he was going to beat me up after school. I didn't pay much attention until he came with a group of his friends to find me after school and escort me to the student parking lot. Being surrounded by his friends and probably 100 other students at the parking lot I felt a little overwhelmed and scared. I felt confident in my ability to defend myself having earned a black-belt in Tae-Kwon-Do, but being a black-belt also taught me self control and not to use my skills to fight others for no good reason. I tried to talk my way out of a fight, but the crowd was blood thirsty and kept egging the bully on. The bully finally started the fight by punching me in the chin. I responded with a few quick blows to his face and then grabbed him in a headlock to bring him to the ground. He was about 220lbs to my 140lbs. Once I got him in a headlock I continued to hit him in the face. This was a 20 second ordeal and once I realized that I was in the middle of a brutal fight I looked around at a way to get out of the situation. I let him go and he fell back and kicked my eye as he fell. I sprang up and walked away telling him it was over. He still threatened me after that, but never touched me again. We both got suspended, but he was the one with two black eyes and a bruised ego. I can't say he stopped being a bully after that, but he didn't do it around me. I am sure that my brother was picked on in school as well, I just hoped that there were other kids like me around to stand up for them. I also hoped that the school administration would supervise the students and protect the handicapped children better.

I have already mapped out in my mind the future of my sons. They will go to school, play sports, have friends, go on dates, go to college, get married, have a career, and have their own homes. None of that was possible for my brother Scott. So if I were to find out my son was autistic I would have to erase all of that from my mind and be ready for an entirely different future which would be nothing like the other 99% of children. I love my brother and am grateful for having him in my life, but I would never desire anyone to be autistic or have an autistic child. I feel that I have benefited far more from Scott's autism than he has. I don't see any benefits in it for him. I try to keep a positive outlook on my family's life with Scott. So I would just say that although there are some negative impacts on the family the person who is missing out the most is the person who is autistic themselves.

Laura (age 33)

The last time I lived with Scott he hadn't even reached puberty. When I think of how autism has affected my life, I immediately think back to when Scott was first showing symptoms. I was 10 when we started to notice behavior changes, like taking poop out of his diaper and smearing it on the wall. I remember him losing his verbal ability. He actually stopped using words that he had previously used. It was really weird. I remember distinctly going to the hospital to visit Mom when Alison was born, so Scott was almost 25 months old, and Scott freaked out. He was really upset, crying and not wanting to be there at all. It was really hard for me because we had to leave pretty quickly but I wanted to stay and see my new sister who I had been waiting a really long time for.

For the next several years, it was like we had 2 babies with Alison and Scott. I had to grow up fast. In my preteen years, I felt more like a third parent than a child. Scott even called me Mommy for a while. I did enjoy the bond I had with him, though. As I learned more about autism and met other children with autism, it seemed to me that Scott was a lot more affectionate than a lot of other children with autism. He liked to be held and he would snuggle with me.

Although my memories of that time are fuzzy now that so much time has passed, I remember often thinking back then that Mom and Dad changed when Scott was diagnosed. They weren't as happy or carefree as they had previously been. There was a new sadness and seriousness about them. I had a hard time seeing them change like that and I often wished they would return to their previous happiness. Mom and Dad missed a lot of events due to Scott; that was always really hard for me. There were several band and choir concerts that only occurred on one night so usually Mom would come and Dad would stay with Scott.

I remember how someone was always on Scott duty when we went out. Usually that meant actually holding on to him in some way so he wouldn't just run off. And I remember how even at home we were always mindful of where Scott was and what he was doing. I do that now with my children. I am always aware of where they are and what they are doing. I rarely leave them alone for more than a couple of minutes without going to check on them. I wonder if this hyper vigilance is related to my experiences with Scott. I've heard many stories from other mothers about the awful things their young children have gotten into while the mothers were otherwise occupied and I have always wondered how their kids do these things without them knowing. Maybe since they didn't develop that hyper vigilance out of necessity for a family member's safety, they are comfortable leaving their young children unattended. I don't know if there is any link, but I thought it was interesting.

I've also found myself watching my young toddlers closely for any autism-like behavior. Watching my children learn and grow has been one of the greatest joys of being a parent so finding out that their development would be significantly halted would be really hard to deal with.

Even with the hardships and trials that come with having a family member with autism, I am still profoundly grateful that Scott was sent to our family. I am fortunate to have Scott as my brother for many reasons. For one, he taught me while I was still quite young that great sacrifice and service to others can bring great joy. Also, I learned that family relationships can be strengthened as family members face trials together. My parents, siblings, and I have had difficult experiences due to Scott's autism, but those experiences have brought us closer to one another as we have relied on each other for support and have served Scott together. Scott has provided me and the rest of our family with many opportunities to show unconditional love and to grow through performing selfless acts of service. My experiences with Scott have made me a better person. I am more patient, more understanding and tolerant of differences, more aware of the hardships that people face when caring for a loved one who is ill or has a disability, and more willing to serve those in need. I hope that my small acts of service for Scott have made his life a little better, too. I love my brother!

Paul Brodie

6. Autism's Effect on me

As I have already mentioned, it is difficult to define my life in terms of with or without autism. I was six and a half when Scott was born, which made me nine when he was diagnosed with PDD-NOS. I remember getting picked up from elementary school by my dad one afternoon. He told us about Scott's diagnosis. That is all I recall from the moment, just a few frames in my mind. I don't know if that was for the PDD-NOS diagnosis or for autism two years later. Another early memory of autism creeping into my life was at school, standing in line in the hallway, waiting to go somewhere. I was talking to my best friend; it must have been Jeff based on the timing of the diagnosis of autism. I recall telling him that my brother was autistic. He said something to the effect of, "That's cool, so he can draw really well or something?" I said, "*Autistic*, not *artistic*." And thus began my life of trying to understand autism and explain it to others.

As a child I didn't understand autism and I didn't know how to relate to my brother. None of us did, so we all had to work it out on our own. There weren't any training manuals for my parents, let alone us kids. Sadly, I think I avoided Scott a lot. I was an active participant in caring for him, like everyone in the family was, but beyond doing things for him I didn't know how to do things with him. I would try, but without reciprocity I really struggled. Things changed as I matured, but it was still easier to do things for him than to do things with him. I often feel guilty about that. Living with Scott has helped me increase in tolerance, compassion, patience and understanding and hopefully selflessness as well, but this last one still stands in need of improvement.

I was always shy as a child, and the shyness didn't burn off as I entered adulthood. In some ways it became more difficult. The diagnosis-crazed era between the late 20th and early 21st centuries labeled me with generalized anxiety disorder (I suppose I'm participating in the diagnosis-craze by inventing the term secondhand autism). I don't know if any of those issues I dealt with were directly related to autism in the home or not, but my problems certainly affected how I interacted with Scott. Being in public was difficult for me because I had irrational thoughts and fears of attention. I didn't like it if I didn't feel I could control it, and often I didn't feel like I could control attention from other people. This made it extremely difficult for me to take Scott anywhere, just me and him, or to be with him at all in public as he often invited attention. My anxiety would engage and though I know the attention was on him, in the moment I couldn't think like that and I would be painfully uncomfortable. Thankfully I've been able to work through the anxiety pretty well for myself, but even now, at 31, married, a father, years of work experience and a graduate degree, I still feel anxious thinking about taking Scott somewhere by myself.

This anxiety is partly due to my own physiological and mental composition, but it is also the result of the hyper vigilance and awareness I developed in relation to Scott because of the autism. At night when my daughter cries I'm often standing up out of bed before I realize she is crying and I'm awake. I guess I'm a light sleeper. Having lived under lockdown conditions at home, needing a key to access any part of the house, or to leave the house, I still obsessively check and recheck locks on doors. I pay attention to everything, and think through everything. These aren't always bad things, and I think in some cases they are beneficial, but they are symptoms of secondhand autism. When I see these traits expressed in my parents, however, I don't see them quite so favorably. My parents are constantly worried and anxious about what Scott is doing, where he is, whether the appropriate locks are engaged, etc. I still have moments of worry and obsession which I attribute to living with autism, but for my parents it is constant. I worry about the effect on their health. Autism isn't communicable, but it does have collateral damage.

One of the worries that lie dormant in my mind, surfacing briefly every now and then, is that my children will be autistic. I don't worry about anything else for them, at least as far as diseases or disabilities go, those aren't even on my radar. I do worry about the state of public education and plan to pursue home schooling, but that's another story. Scott has a repetitive behavior of biting his right hand between his thumb and index finger. The skin on the back of his hand has a crescent moon shaped callus unlike any callus I've ever seen before. He has done this biting behavior for his entire life. My daughter is just under a year old and she often bites her hand in the same way, but only briefly and quickly moves her hand around either to suck on her fingers or to move her hand in and out of her mouth manipulating the sound of her singing. Every time her hand is in that position in her mouth I think about Scott and worry that Megan will be autistic. I have no other evidence to charge this to, and she is still young, but each time I see the behavior I think the same thing.

I've heard that siblings of autistic children will express autistic-like traits. I don't know the evidence behind that claim or if it is valid, but I do know that I tend to perseverate on things like Scott does. Maybe not the same way he does, but I tend to develop a narrow focus or a persistent thought about something for a long time.

Maybe it is normal; I've never discussed it with anyone or come across it in reading, so I attribute it to an autistic-like trait. Scott sometimes gets his mind on something and seems like he can't be deterred from carrying it out, often this is in gaining access to candy or a movie he wants to watch. At times he clearly becomes agitated over his inability to get what he wants. He'll stay obsessed over it until he gets it. While in my case the agitation isn't a part of it, I do become fixed on an idea until it is resolved.

For example, not long ago something spurred a memory recollection of a candy I used to get at *Jamesway* (a pre-*Walmart* department store in NJ) when I was a kid. The store had a metal wire candy display with assorted types of individually wrapped candy in baskets. There was a metal box with a padlock on it where you would insert a quarter and then you could take a piece of candy, or you could bag a bunch up and take it to a checkout clerk. Jelly nougat was the one I liked to get. I think it was just before last Christmas when my wife and I were looking through a candy recipe book thinking up ideas of what to make. There was a recipe for nougat. I remembered the candy and from then on I would occasionally have the thought come to my mind that I wanted to find the jelly nougat candy I hadn't seen for probably twenty years. I looked for it at every store we visited for two months. The thought just hung around in my mind. Finally I thought to check Amazon.com and they had it. I bought a bag, which sits near the computer now, largely untouched. It wasn't so much that I wanted the candy anymore as that I needed to resolve the thought. This happens in regards to food, movies, songs, talking to people and activities. Something gets in my mind and it stays bobbing around the surface of consciousness until I resolve it. I can't know for sure if this is an autistic-like trait, if it is induced in me because of Scott's autism or if it is anything close to what Scott experiences, but this is how I define it.

Secondhand Autism

Between my own experiences with anxiety and my firsthand exposure to autism, when I made the decision to pursue a university education I was drawn towards psychology. I never really understood what psychology was or what a career in psychology really entailed until I began classes. I found I really enjoyed learning about how the body works, especially the brain. I learned a lot that helped me to understand autism and life influenced by it. Even though my study was never specifically focused on autism outside a brief section in an abnormal psychology class, random mentions in a neuro-psych class and one class called "Autism" hosted by the special education department at my university, the information I learned all seemed to relate to my understanding of life and autism. It wasn't that the focus of the classes was autism related; rather my focus in general was and in some ways continues to be aimed at autism. The class on autism was very influential for me because it taught me how expansive the autism spectrum is.

There were twelve students in the class, it was pretty small. All but one of the students had a sibling, cousin, nephew or niece, or was diagnosed themselves with ASD. This brought twelve unique experiences and perceptions regarding autism to the discussions. I often felt frustrated and my chip-on-the-shoulder attitude really became clear. No one there knew autism like I knew it, and I often told my classmates as much. I wish I would have been more understanding. The same carousel of emotion has influenced how I've typed this book, at times I hate autism and at times I appreciate its influence on me. Participating in that class taught me that bias suppression regarding autism would be a difficult thing for me if I ever entered a career path that would require it. My perception of autism influenced me deeply even though I was two thousand miles away from my brother, it had been a year or more since I'd lived at home and I was in an academic setting. Autism has influenced my perception and permeated every bit of who I am.

My wife is from Utah; we were married in Utah. After everyone flying to California for John's wedding we decided not to take Scott to Utah for my wedding. This meant dad stayed home, too. Autism didn't prevent my dad and Scott from attending my wedding, but it heavily influenced the decision to do it the way we did. When we flew with Scott to California it was difficult keeping tabs on him in the airport and Scott seemed very uncomfortable on the plane during take-off and landing. Even with the sedative the doctor had prescribed for the plane ride. I would have liked to have had them there, but I understood the difficulty of making the trip. Autism is more than the physical things. We have all developed different ways of thinking about life and placing value on things. Sometimes things just are what they are, you adapt to them and continue on, or you give up and lie down. My parents have shown me that nothing is so bad that you should just give up and lie down; you always adapt and overcome the situation. I wanted Scott and dad at my wedding, but functionally it wasn't feasible, so they weren't there. Neither was Laura or her family as she had just given birth to their second child a few weeks earlier. So it isn't always autism that interferes with life's plans, but it is autism that makes me not lose sleep over disappointments, such as half my family not being able to attend my wedding.

I suppose if I were to narrow down autism's effect on me to one word it would be awareness. I am more aware because of autism. I'm aware of my brother and what he is doing when I'm around him, but I am also aware of how I feel autism has cheated our family, primarily my brother, out of normal experiences. At the same time I am aware of the benefits we have all gained by virtue of the challenges presented by autism. I am aware that I dislike autism and that I appreciate its effects. I am aware that my physical awareness of whatever environment I am in is heightened. I am aware that we cannot divorce ourselves from certain experiences, and that those experiences become a part of what we are in much the same way that the food we eat becomes the substance of the cells of our bodies. My brother Scott is diagnosed with autistic disorder, but our whole family is autistic.

In the context of this book it sounds like I can do nothing without thinking about autism, but this isn't the case at all. The constant influence is there, as I said, by being part of the fabric of my personal development over the years. My subconscious mind likely reflects this most without my conscious awareness of it. Certain words and behaviors trigger my mind to recall to the forefront images of autism's influence in my family, but for the most part I just live. Autism is a tag in memories and interactions with my family on an ongoing basis, and although it does define us, it is up to us to define it.

7. The Secondhand Autism Prognosis

The Despair and the Hope

The biggest hope is that autism will be cured, and the greatest despair is that it won't happen in time for my child (in my personal case, my brother). Hope comes easily, I think, for parents of autistic children, but primarily in regards only to their child overcoming autism. Beyond that hope it is difficult to have hope in the face of the failed toilet training efforts until the child is 6 or 7, the inconsolable crying spells, the picky eating, the sensitivity to light and sound and the utter lack of communication. The constant worrying and hyper vigilance, the concern over the effect of constant stress on the marriage and the reduced time to spend with other children can become very depressing. Books, blogs, websites, TV interviews and word of mouth all combine to generate rumors and false hope of miraculous cures for autism. But autism is especially unique. Autism for one child is different from autism for another child. With a preponderance of autistic-like symptoms and the wide range of classification of ASD there are many claims of therapeutic cure that have absolutely no positive effect on one child or another. These stories fuel the hope, but also the despair.

A heavy concern that weighs on aging parents is the ability to provide the same level of care for their autistic child as that child becomes an adult and as their strength diminishes with age. My parents share this concern. They do not look fondly on the idea of turning Scott's care over to agencies and the State, but they know they will not be able to care for him in the same capacity forever. They also don't want to turn Scott over to one of their other children because they know the impact an adult autistic man would have on the lives of their grandchildren, Scott's nephews and nieces. Personally, I am conflicted on the issue. I believe Scott will always be better off living with his own family members, and if that causes stress on our families, that's part of our family responsibility and I hope that I can exercise the same strength, or even a portion of it, that I have seen my parents exhibit. On the other hand, there may be a situation where having Scott live in an assisted living home may be more ideal for him based on the services he'd have access to than if he was living in the home of one of his siblings' families. What do we do as Scott gets older, but his level of self care and functioning don't improve? That is the big question we occasionally think about, but dread the day when the decision needs to be made.

There is no doubt that autism is difficult to deal with. It is a constant struggle involving the entire family. People either adapt to it and work all day every day, or they give up and run away from the responsibility. A lot of the decision depends on long term outlook and personal philosophy. My family is very involved with Christianity. For us, hope and peace come through the teachings of Jesus Christ and the eternal hope that all of our struggles during life will work together to make us better individuals in the long run. We believe in an eternal family, where even after this life we will exist in a similar fashion with our current relationships and experiences. In that time there will be no autism, no anxiety, no depression; there will only be peace and joy. This concept of belief may be difficult for some to embrace; others might dismiss it entirely as delusional or out of bounds with reality. I encourage everyone to develop their own personal set of beliefs to draw strength from. We don't all have to believe the same things, but I hope that everyone believes in something greater than self. I believe that is the first step to understanding what can and can't be controlled in life, which helps give appropriate meaning to experience and aids in dismissing the thoughts that are most depressing. Our family may have lost hope of Scott's recovery from autism many years ago, but we maintain the hope of being with him in perfected form after our mortal experience is over.

Autism is for Life

There is no cure for autism. There is no known cause of autism. If you search for them, you can find cases of cures and alleged causes, but officially there is no universal answer for either. Perhaps this is because autism is so individual. Maybe there is a genetic link that only manifests as autism under the right conditions, or wrong, depending on how you view it. It may be that the cured cases of autism were autistic-like symptoms brought on by allergies, thereby resolution of the symptoms occur with removal of the allergen. It could be possible that an allergy, or an individual body's inability to process or generate certain chemicals, could block or hinder normal development in the brain.

Environmental factors could also do it. This isn't to say that the "refrigerator mother" theory is legitimate, but absolute neglect of a child may result in autistic-like traits. The problem with the "refrigerator mother" theory was that it said all mothers of autistic children were responsible, against the evidence that there were mothers who were doing all they possibly could to connect with their children. However, parental neglect can lead to cognitive delay and dysfunction. In the terribly sad instance of feral children there have been cases where verbal communication was impossible to teach after years of trying. A child who lives without any human interaction can develop brain atrophy, or non-development, which manifests in similar symptoms to autism. When children have been found after they experienced years of social deprivation and isolation they seemed developmentally damned in certain regards, especially verbal communication. Environmental factors can lead to autistic-like traits.

I believe that whatever the origin of autism, something effects the development of the brain at critical moments. Depending on when those critical moments are, and what type of intervention is pursued, sometimes autistic symptoms can be averted or reduced. But it is strictly "sometimes" and in "some cases." As discouraging as it may sound, I think for most true instances of autism, autism is for life. I don't see a day when my brother will ever talk with me like I can talk with our other siblings. Nor can I foresee a time when he won't need to be locked in the house to prevent him from heading out in search of a store, or store advertisements in people's mailboxes. If there was a time to prevent his symptoms, I think it is past. Maybe there never was a time at all. It all depends on where autism comes from. If it is genetic then it likely is what it is. If it is environmental then perhaps there is a possibility for improvement, unless that window of opportunity is already closed.

Secondhand Autism is not Terminal

You can't die from secondhand autism. For one thing, it doesn't exist, I just made it up, but also it is simply a term to refer to the effect that autism has on a family member of an autistic person. It may very well be that genetic factors leading to autism in one child also affect the other children in a family in less severe ways, but I don't know. It may be that the stress induced by caring for an autistic family member will increase susceptibility to health problems in the future, but once again, I don't know. Secondhand autism is less about the physical effects on family members than the emotional and personality effects. Because secondhand autism defines the influence of autism on how a family member lives, it will exist throughout the person's life. Autism does not typically include any shortened life expectancy, nor does secondhand autism. As for whether this should be encouraging or discouraging all depends on the meaning you find in it.

Finding Meaning in the Disorder

As I've been writing this book I have engaged my family in discussions about the topic and requested written notes from them about their memories and experiences. The phrase "our family is defined by autism" has come up. Through our lives we have been heavily influenced by autism, there is no doubt about that. Every aspect of life somehow relates to autism, not so much for those of us grown up and out of the house, but when we were all home together it seemed there was nothing that was out of the reaches of autism. To an extent our family is defined by autism, but what I've come to realize is that we define autism in our family. When I think about autism I either become frustrated or peaceful. Autism in my mind is a great challenge, and as I have explained there are many factors that contribute to the challenge and lead to my frustration. At other times I find peace as I think about autism because I consider my personal concept of eternity and find that autism, for all of its frustration, is as the refiner's fire in an eternal perspective.

No discussion on finding meaning in life, especially through trying times, is complete without mentioning Viktor Frankl. Frankl wrote about his experience as a victim of Hitler's Germany in his 1946 work, *Man's Search for Meaning*. I don't compare autism with the Holocaust, but if Frankl could find positive meaning through his experience in Nazi death camps, we can all find meaning in whatever difficult events we encounter. They will be trying, frustrating and push us to our individual limits, but these types of experiences can help us become something better. Frankl knew it and built a fine career and personal reputation on it. We can all find meaning in the difficult aspects of life. If we don't define them then they just might define us. My family is defined by autism, but we are not autism. Scott has autism; though we say he is autistic, in the eternal perspective our family embraces he has it only. In my moments of frustration I might say autism has Scott, and I want him back, but I believe he has it, and after our mortal experience is passed I will know him and he will know me, free from all of our disabilities and flaws we currently hold.

Scott holds autism for the duration of his life, but the flaws I hold don't have to be for that long. Scott's autism has given our family the constant opportunity to serve and grow. Because Scott has autism, I have been able to let go of some of my flaws. Hopefully it has worked to prevent me from picking up other flaws or compounding the ones that remain. If I did not have an eternal perspective and view autism in my family as a catalyst for character development and improvement I think I would feel consumed with the frustration and anger that occasionally stirs itself up in me, questioning why my brother is trapped inside such a dysfunctional body. In that case secondhand autism would define me, and in a way it would be terminal. Every instance of autism is unique and individual. Every parent and sibling of someone diagnosed with ASD is unique and individual. It is up to each one to find meaning in their family experience and define it.

Appendix

Photos

Scott at John and Valerie's wedding. August 2008

Scott at the beach in Monterey, CA. August 2008

Scott at home, approximately 9-years-old

Scott jumping on the trampoline in the backyard. August 2005

Left to right: (Boys) Scott, John, Paul; (Girls) Alison, Shannon, Laura. 2005

References

Autism Epicenter (2013), accessed March 2013, http://www.autismepicenter.com/history-of-autism.shtml

Autism Society (n.d.), accessed March 2013, http://www.autism-society.org/about-autism/

CDC (2012), accessed March 2013, http://www.cdc.gov/ncbddd/autism/topics.html

Frankl, V.E. (1946), *Man's Search for Meaning*, Beacon Press. Boston, MA

Hartley, S.L., Barker, E.T., Seltzer, M.M., Floyd, F., Greenberg, J., Orsmond, G., Bolt, D. (2010). The relative risk and timing of divorce in families of children with an autism spectrum disorder. *Journal of Family Psychology.* 24(4), 449-457. DOI: 10.1037/a0019847

Kennedy Krieger (2010), accessed March 2013, http://www.kennedykrieger.org/overview/news/80-percent-autism-divorce-rate-debunked-first-its-kind-scientific-study

Laidler, J.R. (2004), accessed March 2013, http://www.autism-watch.org/causes/rm.shtml

WebMD (2012), accessed March 2013, http://www.webmd.com/brain/autism/history-of-autism

Wegner, D. M., Fuller, V. A., & Sparrow, B. (2003). Clever hands: Uncontrolled intelligence in facilitated communication. *Journal of Personality and Social Psychology*, 85(1), 5-19. doi:10.1037/0022-3514.85.1.5